SUPER EASY SONGBOOK

QUEEN

T0088584

Cover photo © Getty Images / Michael Ochs Archives / Stringer

ISBN 978-1-5400-5441-8

Visit Hal Leonard Online at
www.halleonard.com

Contact us:
Hal Leonard
7777 West Bluemound Road
Milwaukee, WI 53213
Email: info@halleonard.com

In Europe, contact:
Hal Leonard Europe Limited
42 Wigmore Street
Marylebone, London, W1U 2RN
Email: info@halleonardeurope.com

In Australia, contact:
Hal Leonard Australia Pty. Ltd.
4 Lentara Court
Cheltenham, Victoria, 3192 Australia
Email: info@halleonard.com.au

Welcome to the *Super Easy Songbook* series!

This unique collection will help you play your favorite songs quickly and easily. Here's how it works:

- Play the simplified melody with your right hand. Letter names appear inside each note to assist you.

- There are no key signatures to worry about! If a sharp ♯ or flat ♭ is needed, it is shown beside the note each time.

- There are no page turns, so your hands never have to leave the keyboard.

- If two notes are connected by a tie ‿, hold the first note for the combined number of beats. (The second note does not show a letter name since it is not re-struck.)

- Add basic chords with your left hand using the provided keyboard diagrams. Chord voicings have been carefully chosen to minimize hand movement.

- The left-hand rhythm is up to you, and chord notes can be played together or separately. Be creative!

- If the chords sound muddy, move your left hand an octave* higher. If this gets in the way of playing the melody, move your right hand an octave higher as well.

  An octave spans eight notes. If your starting note is C, the next C to the right is an octave higher.

———————————————— ALSO AVAILABLE ————————————————

Hal Leonard Student Keyboard Guide HL00296039

Key Stickers HL00100016

Another One Bites the Dust

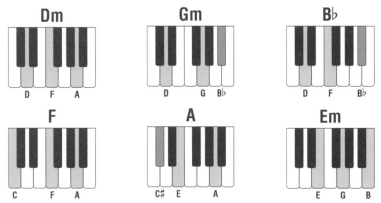

Words and Music by
John Deacon

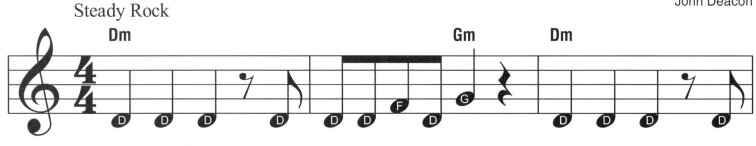

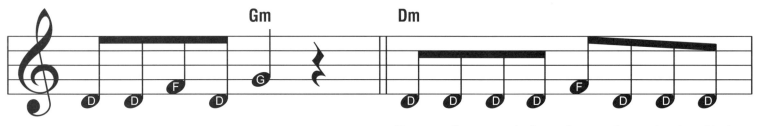

Steve walks war-i-ly down the street with the

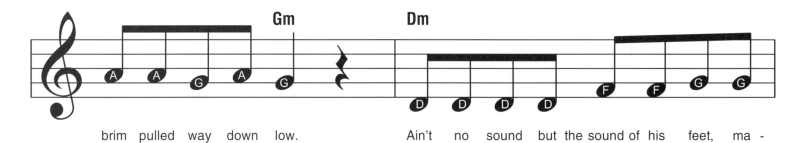

brim pulled way down low. Ain't no sound but the sound of his feet, ma-

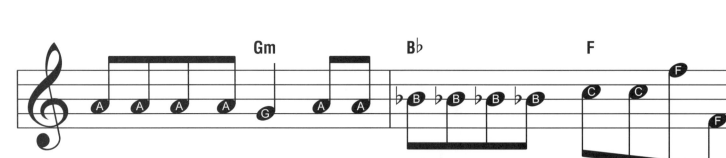

chine guns read-y to go. Are you read-y, hey? Are you read-y for this? Are you

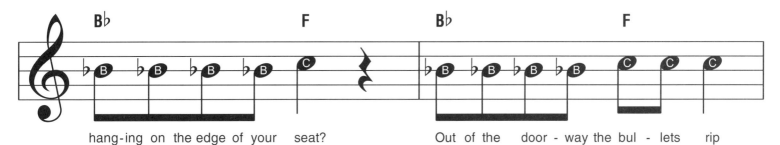

hang-ing on the edge of your seat? Out of the door - way the bul - lets rip

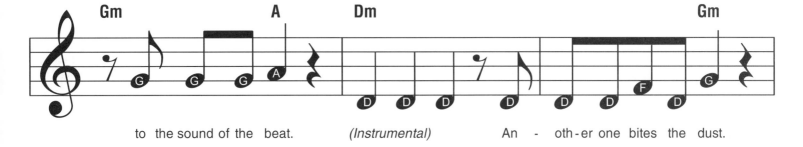

to the sound of the beat. *(Instrumental)* An - oth-er one bites the dust.

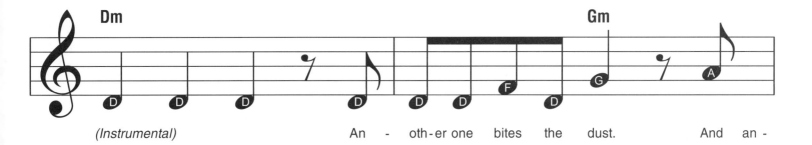

(Instrumental) An - oth-er one bites the dust. And an -

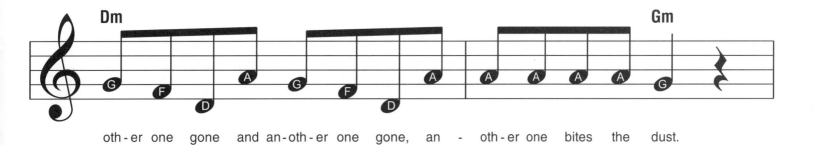

oth - er one gone and an-oth-er one gone, an - oth-er one bites the dust.

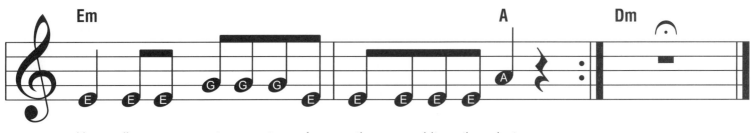

Hey, I'm gon-na get you, too. An - oth-er one bites the dust.

Bohemian Rhapsody

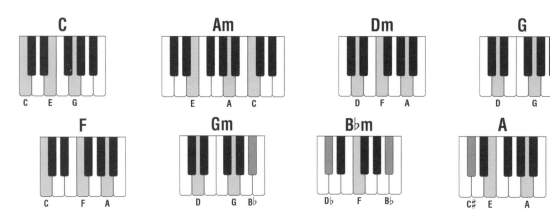

Words and Music by
Freddie Mercury

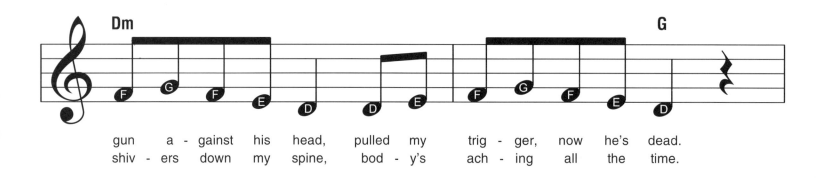

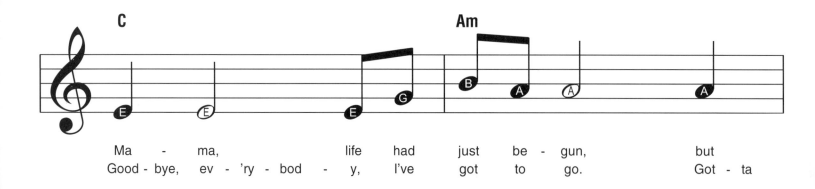

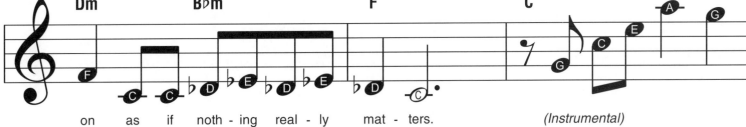

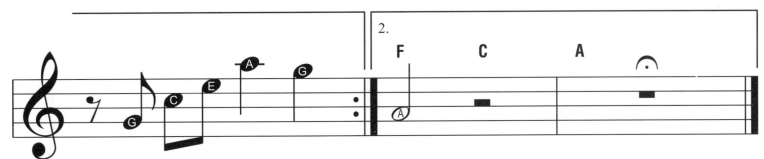

Crazy Little Thing Called Love

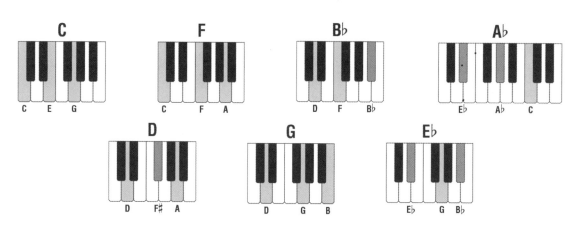

Words and Music by
Freddie Mercury

Moderately fast Shuffle

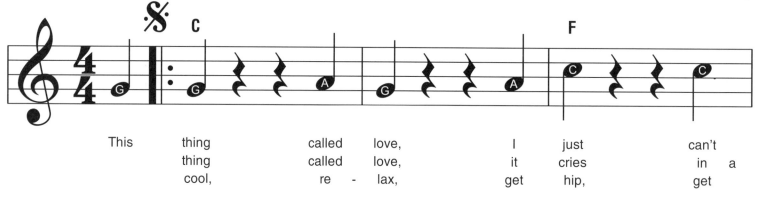

This   thing   called   love,   I   just   can't
thing   called   love,   it   just   cries   in a
cool,   re - lax,   get   hip,   get

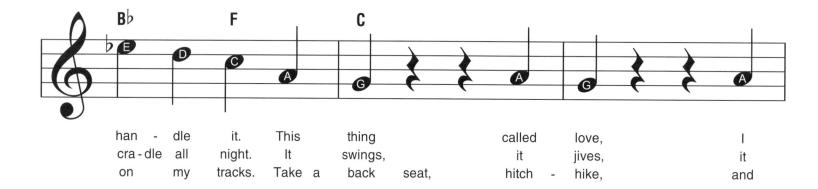

han - dle   it. This   thing   called   love,   I
cra - dle all   night. It   thing   swings,   it   jives,   it
on   my   tracks. Take a   back   seat,   hitch - hike,   and

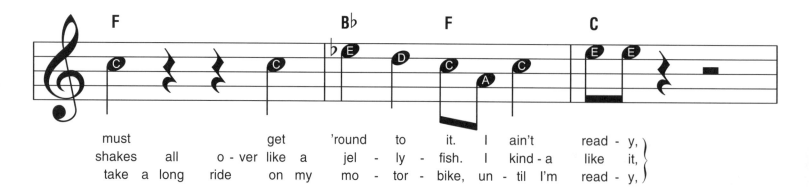

must   get   'round   to   it.   I   ain't   read - y,
shakes   all   o - ver like a   jel - ly - fish. I   kind - a   like it,
take a long   ride   on   my   mo - tor - bike, un - til I'm   read - y,

Doing All Right

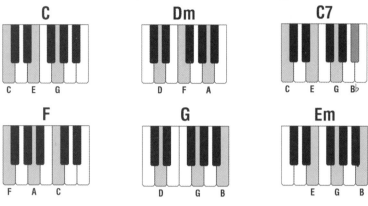

Words and Music by Brian May
and Tim Staffell

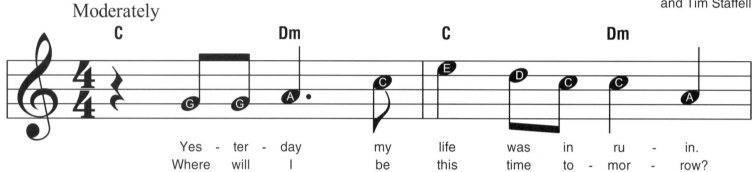

Yes - ter - day my life was in ru - in.
Where will I be this time to - mor - row?

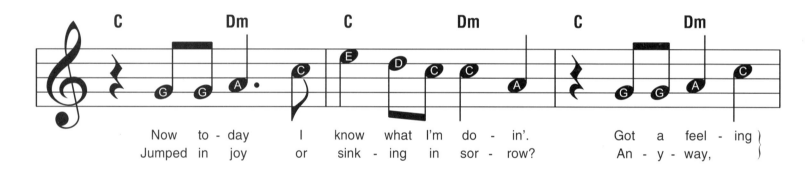

Now to - day I know what I'm do - in'. Got a feel - ing
Jumped in joy or sink - ing in sor - row? An - y - way,

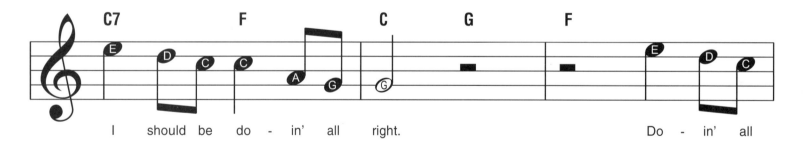

I should be do - in' all right. Do - in' all

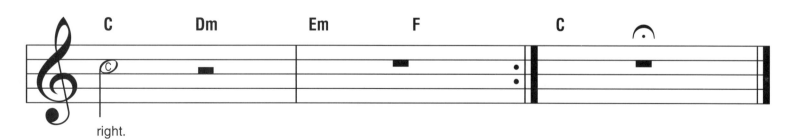

right.

Now I'm Here

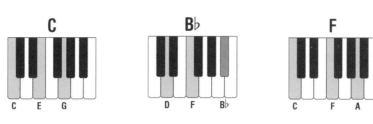
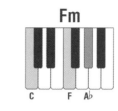

Words and Music by
Brian May

Don't Stop Me Now

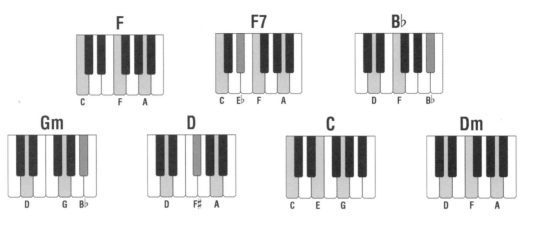

Words and Music by
Freddie Mercury

Moderately fast

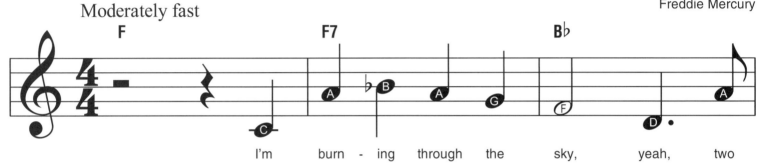

I'm burn - ing through the sky, yeah, two

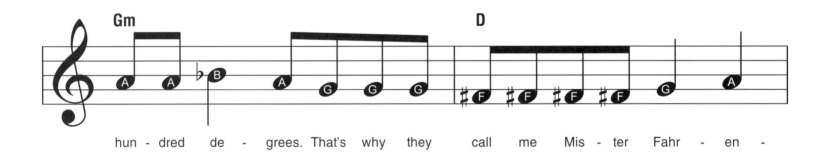

hun - dred de - grees. That's why they call me Mis - ter Fahr - en -

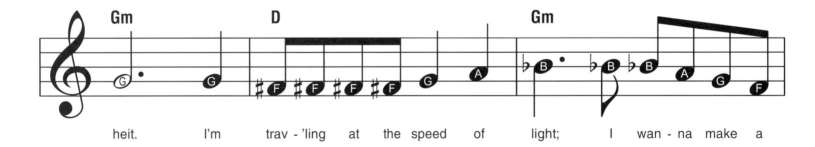

heit. I'm trav - 'ling at the speed of light; I wan - na make a

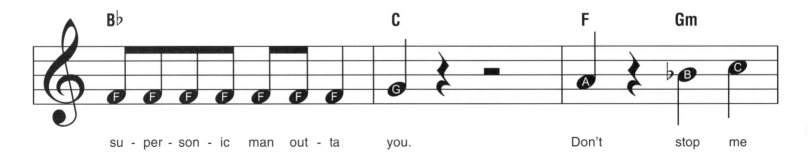

su - per - son - ic man out - ta you. Don't stop me

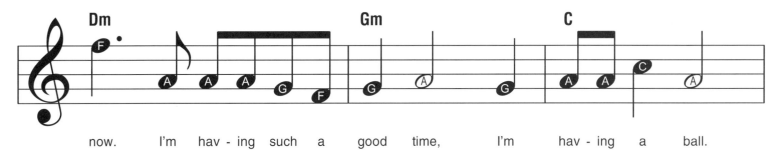

now. I'm hav - ing such a good time, I'm hav - ing a ball.

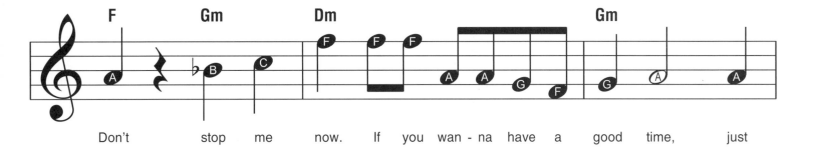

Don't stop me now. If you wan - na have a good time, just

give me a call. Don't stop me, 'cause I'm hav - ing a good time.

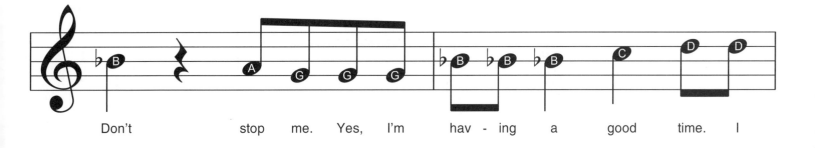

Don't stop me. Yes, I'm hav - ing a good time. I

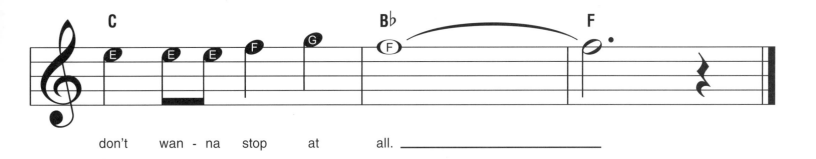

don't wan - na stop at all. _____

Fat Bottomed Girls

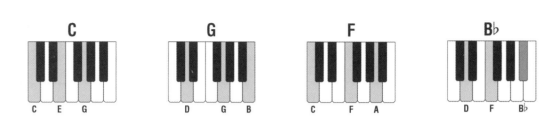

Words and Music by
Brian May

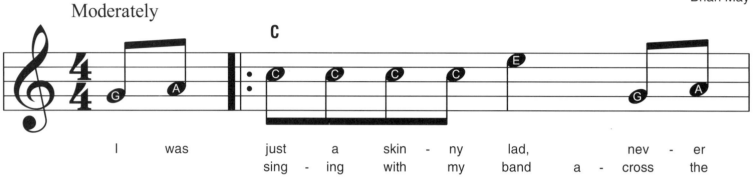

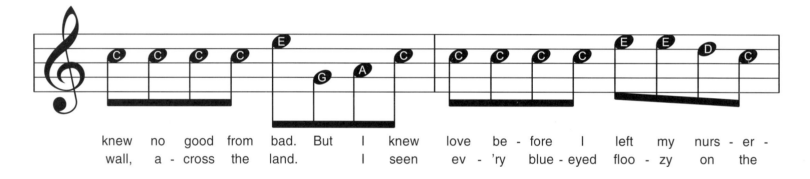

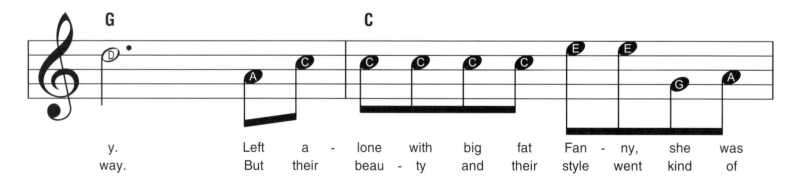

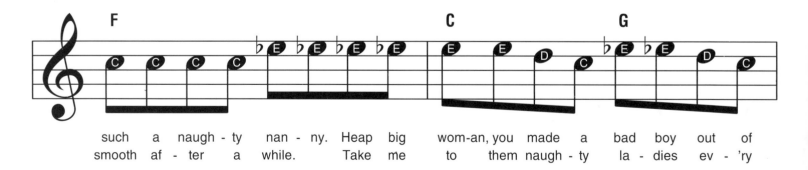

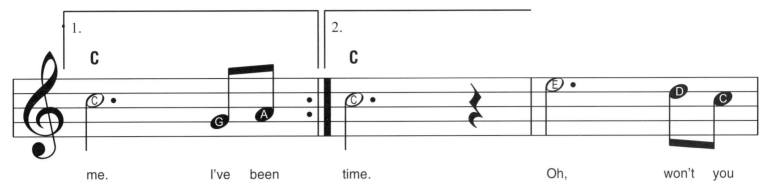

me. I've been time. Oh, won't you

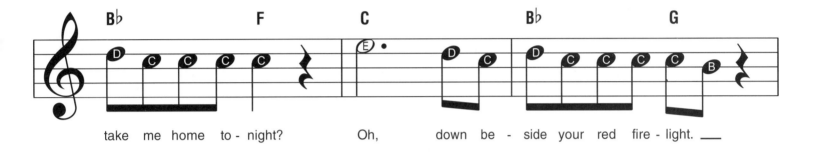

take me home to - night? Oh, down be - side your red fire - light. ___

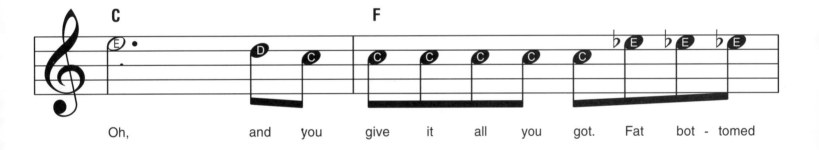

Oh, and you give it all you got. Fat bot - tomed

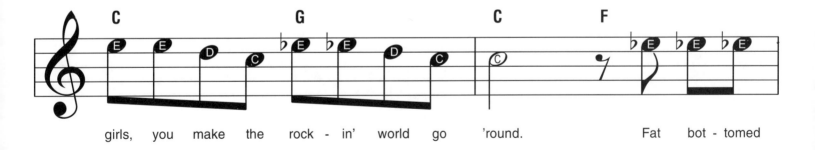

girls, you make the rock - in' world go 'round. Fat bot - tomed

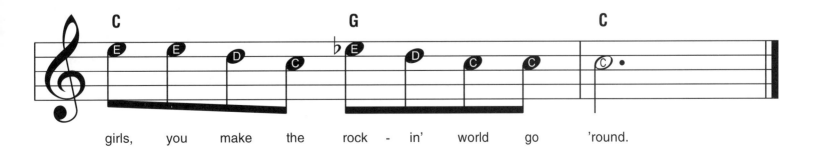

girls, you make the rock - in' world go 'round.

Hammer to Fall

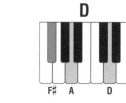

Words and Music by
Brian May

Moderate Rock

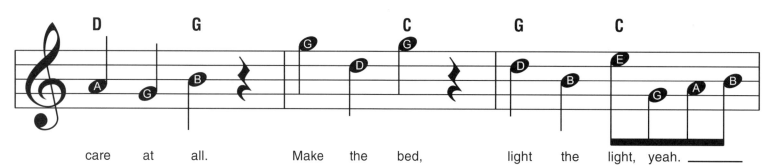

Here we stand and here we fall. His - to - ry won't

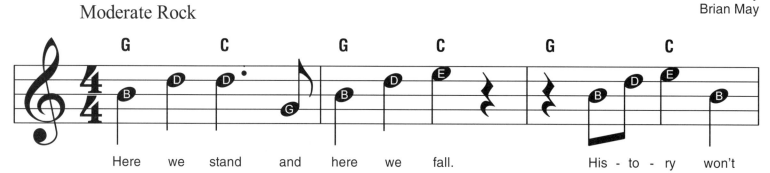

care at all. Make the bed, light the light, yeah. _____

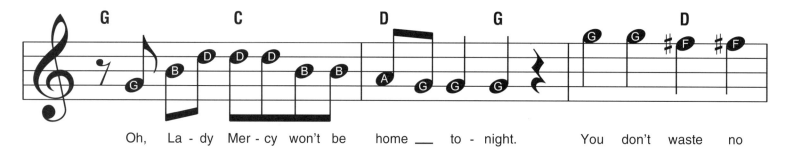

Oh, La - dy Mer - cy won't be home ___ to - night. You don't waste no

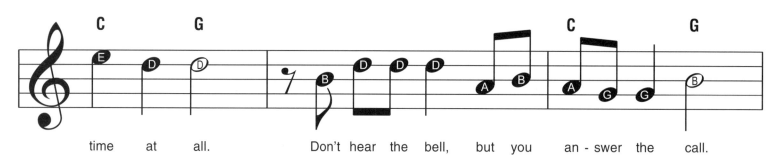

time at all. Don't hear the bell, but you an - swer the call.

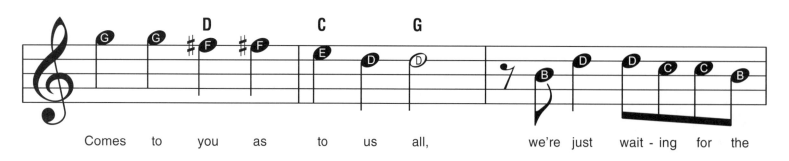

Comes to you as to us all, we're just wait - ing for the

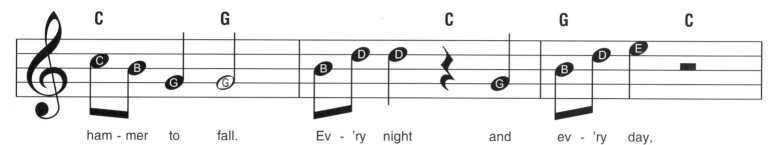

ham - mer to fall. Ev - 'ry night and ev - 'ry day,

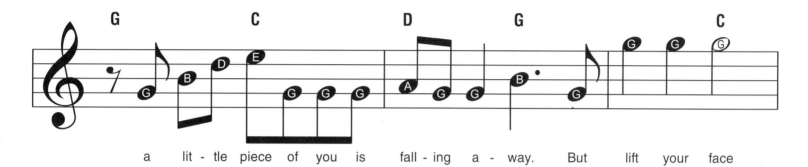

a lit - tle piece of you is fall - ing a - way. But lift your face

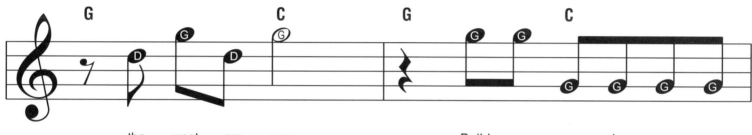

the west - ern way. Build your mus - cles as your

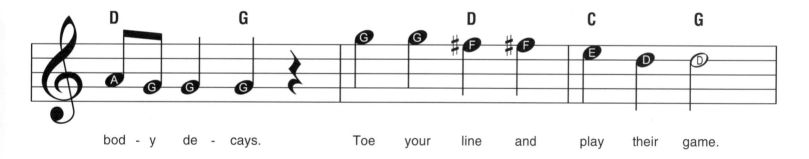

bod - y de - cays. Toe your line and play their game.

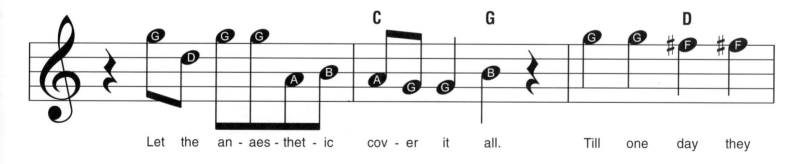

Let the an - aes - thet - ic cov - er it all. Till one day they

call your name. You know it's time for the ham - mer to fall.

I Want to Break Free

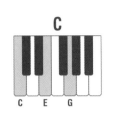

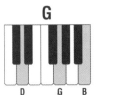
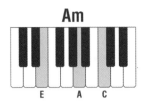
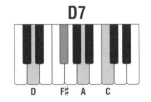

Words and Music by
John Deacon

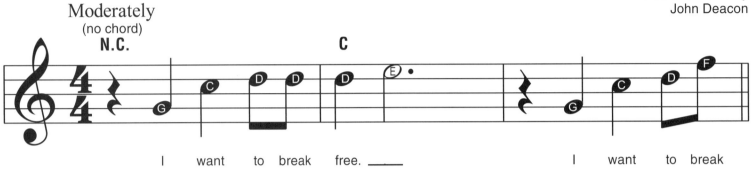

I want to break free. _____ I want to break

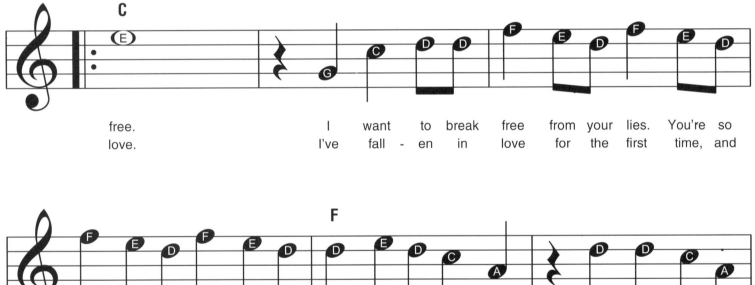

free. _____ I want to break free from your lies. You're so
love. I've fall - en in love for the first time, and

self - sat - is - fied. I don't need _____ you. _____ I've got to break
this time I know it's for real. _____ I've fall - en in

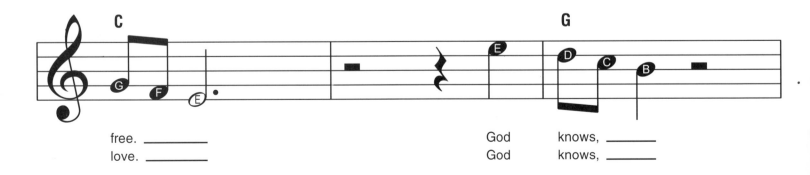

free. _____ God knows, _____
love. _____ God knows, _____

Keep Yourself Alive

Words and Music by
Brian May

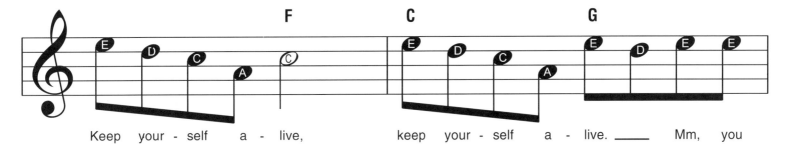

Keep your - self a - live, keep your - self a - live. _____ Mm, you

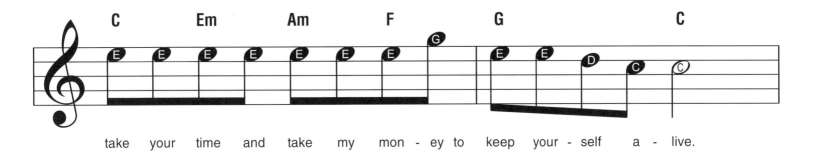

take your time and take my mon - ey to keep your - self a - live.

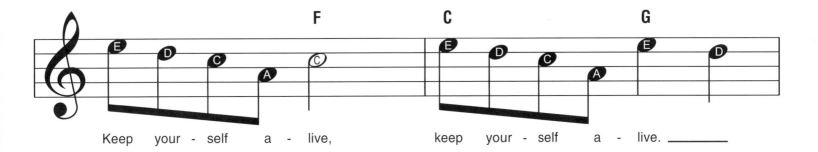

Keep your - self a - live, keep your - self a - live. _____

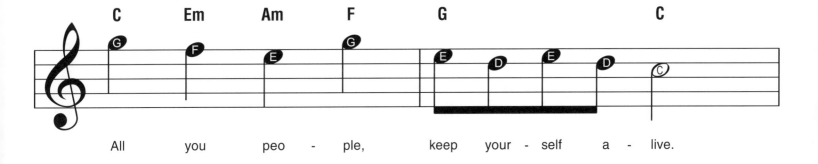

All you peo - ple, keep your - self a - live.

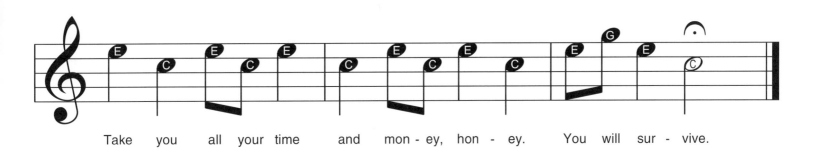

Take you all your time and mon - ey, hon - ey. You will sur - vive.

Killer Queen

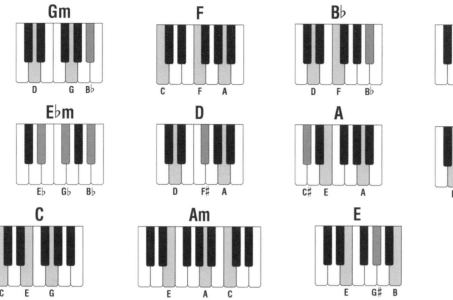

Words and Music by
Freddie Mercury

Moderate Shuffle

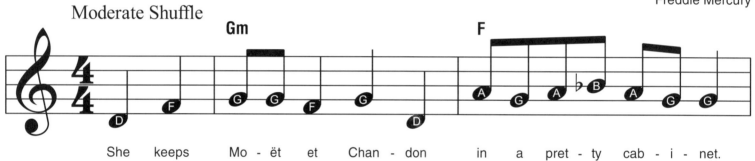

She keeps Mo-ët et Chan-don in a pret-ty cab-i-net.

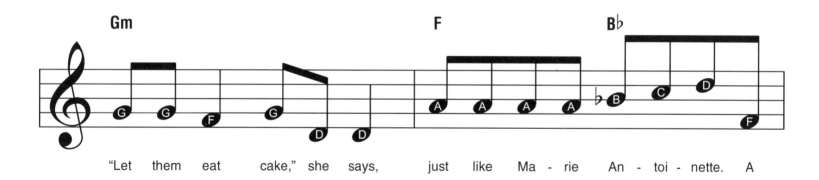

"Let them eat cake," she says, just like Ma-rie An-toi-nette. A

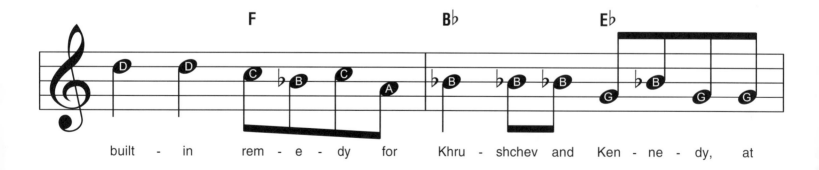

built-in rem-e-dy for Khru-shchev and Ken-ne-dy, at

Love of My Life

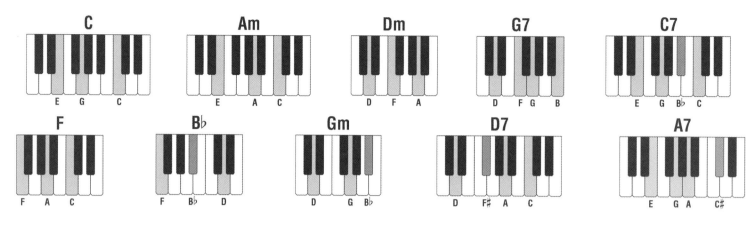

Words and Music by
Freddie Mercury

Moderately slow

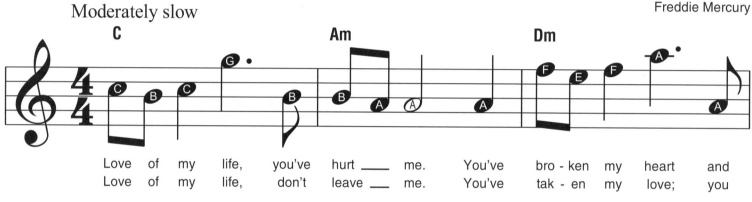

Love of my life, you've hurt ___ me. You've bro - ken my heart and
Love of my life, don't leave ___ me. You've tak - en my love; you

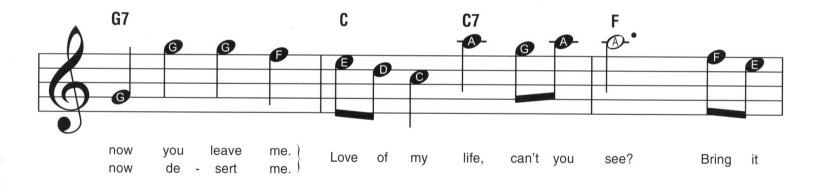

now you leave me. Love of my life, can't you see? Bring it
now de - sert me.

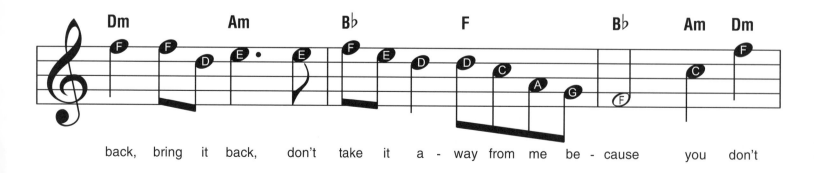

back, bring it back, don't take it a - way from me be - cause you don't

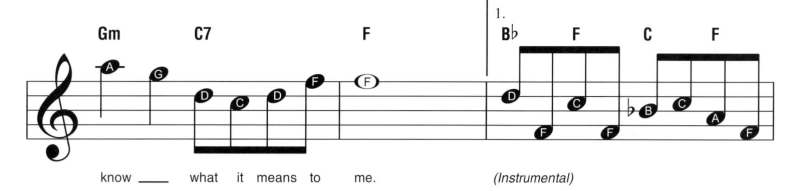

know _____ what it means to me. *(Instrumental)*

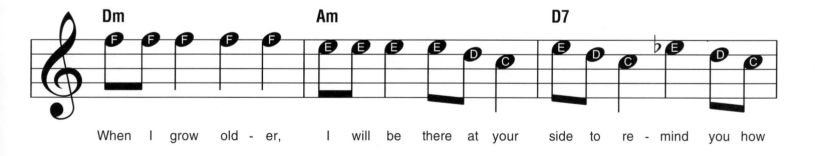

You'll re - mem - ber when

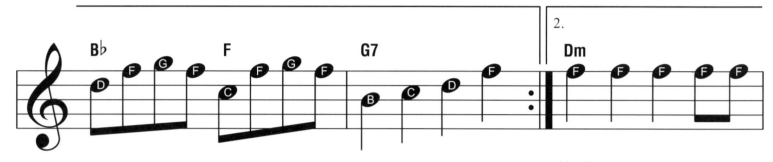

this is blown o - ver and ev - 'ry - thing's all by the way.

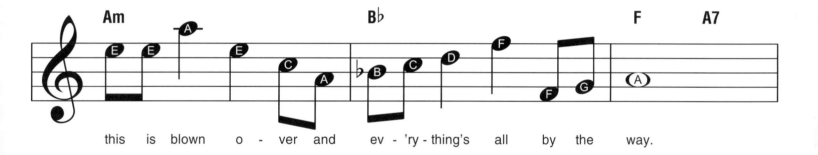

When I grow old - er, I will be there at your side to re - mind you how

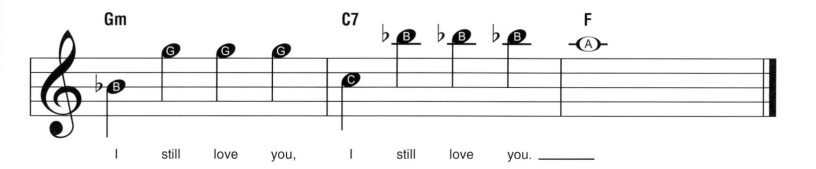

I still love you, I still love you. _____

Radio Ga Ga

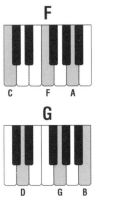
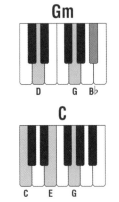
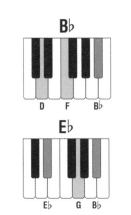
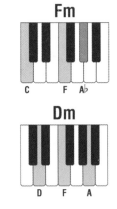

Words and Music by
Roger Taylor

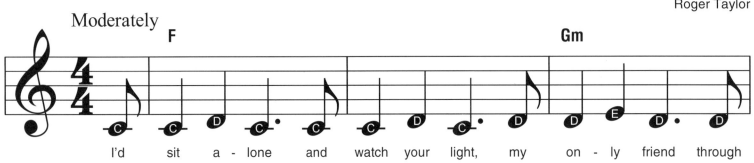

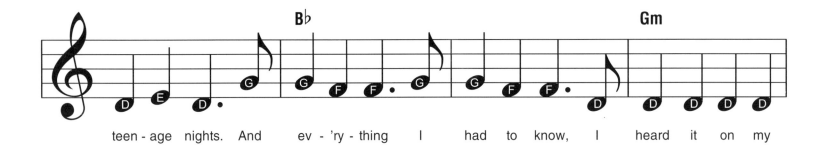

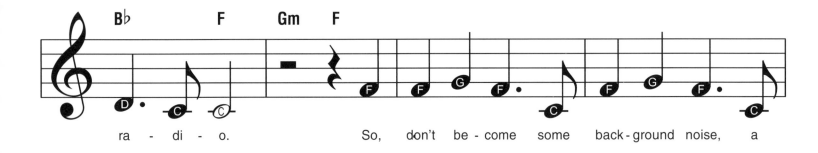

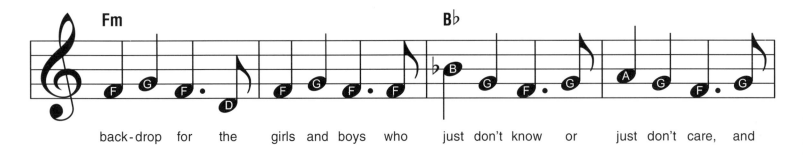

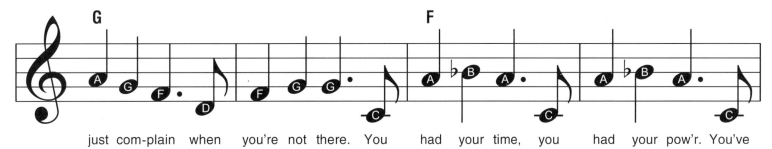

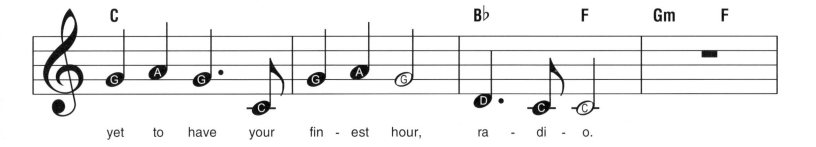

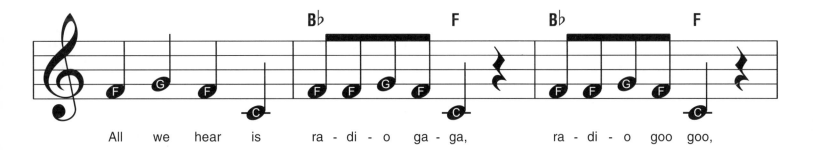

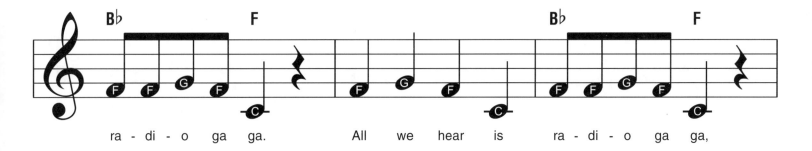

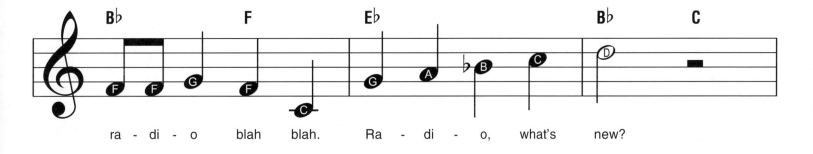

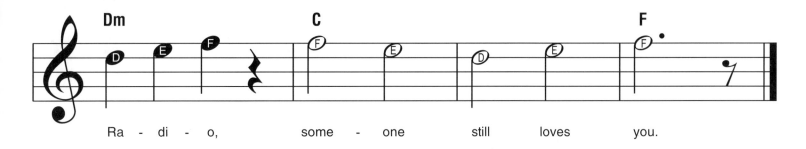

The Show Must Go On

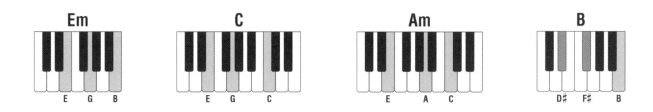

Words and Music by Freddie Mercury,
Brian May, Roger Taylor
and John Deacon

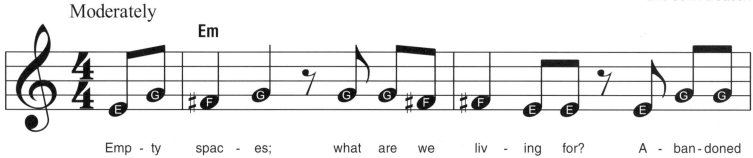

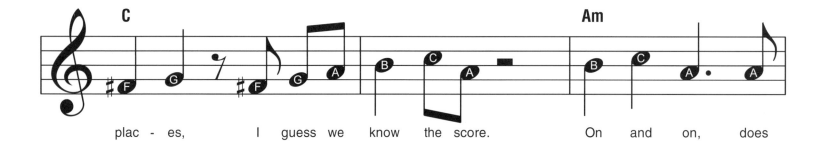

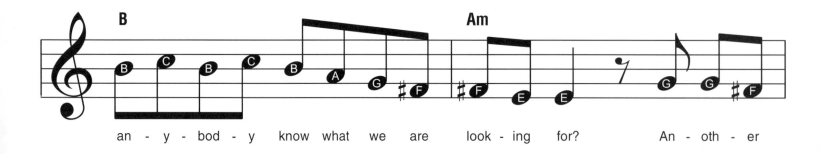

he - ro, an - oth - er mind - less crime, be - hind the cur - tain in the

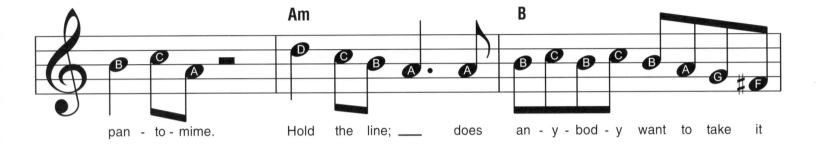

pan - to - mime. Hold the line; ____ does an - y - bod - y want to take it

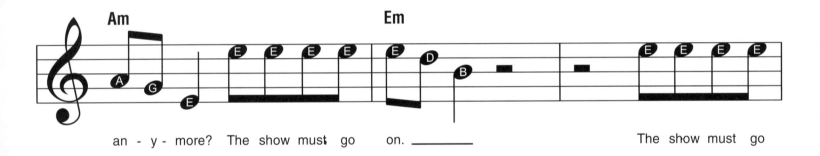

an - y - more? The show must go on. _____ The show must go

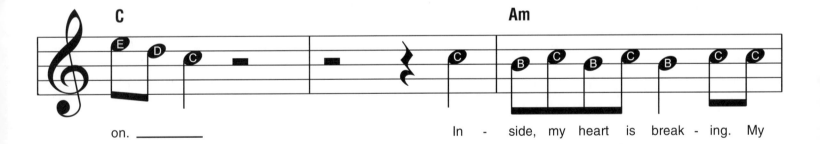

on. _____ In - side, my heart is break - ing. My

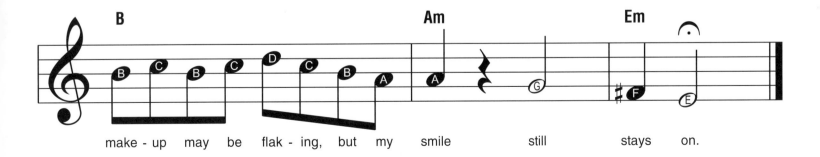

make - up may be flak - ing, but my smile still stays on.

Somebody to Love

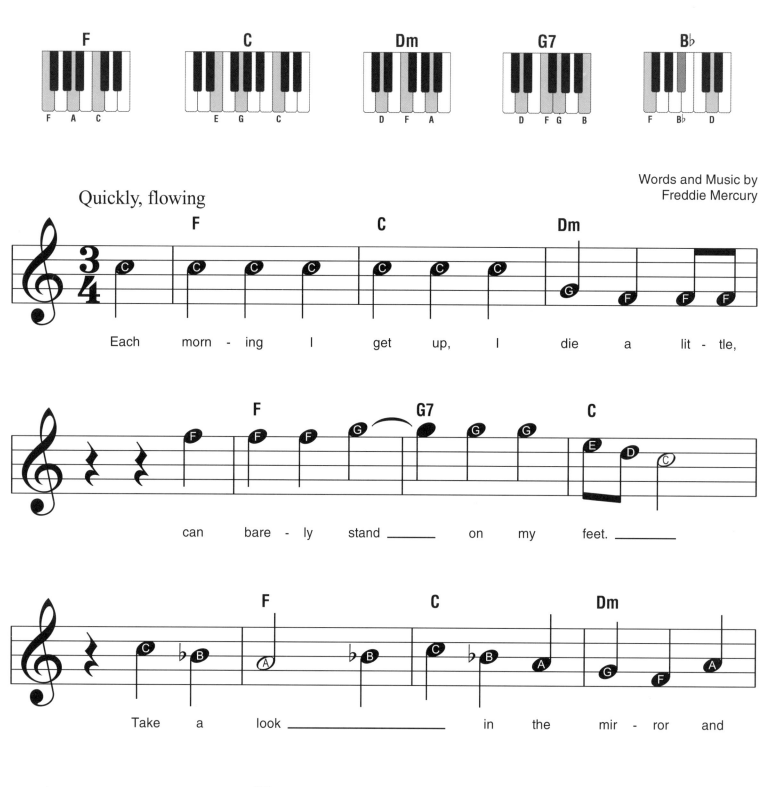

Words and Music by
Freddie Mercury

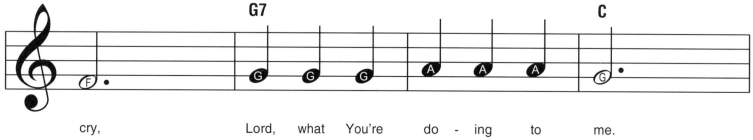

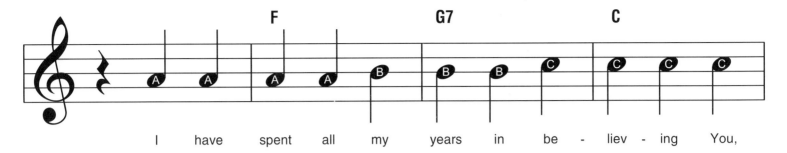

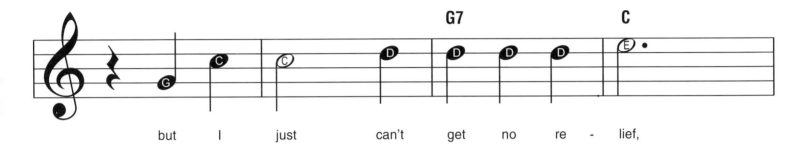

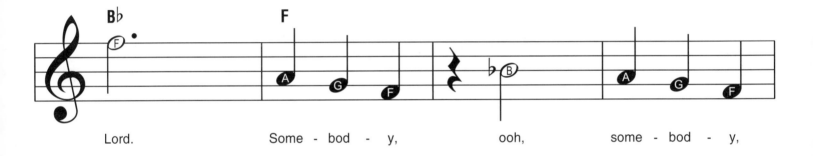

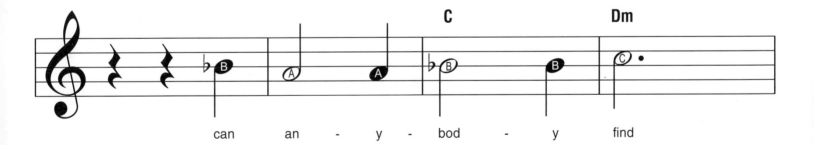

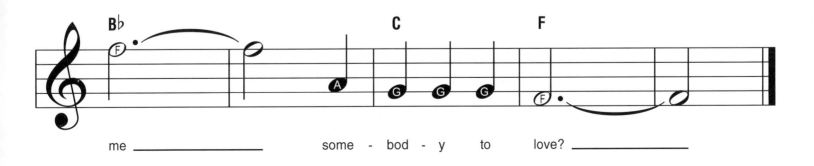

Under Pressure

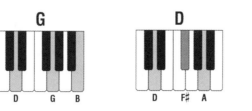
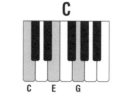

Words and Music by Freddie Mercury,
John Deacon, Brian May,
Roger Taylor and David Bowie

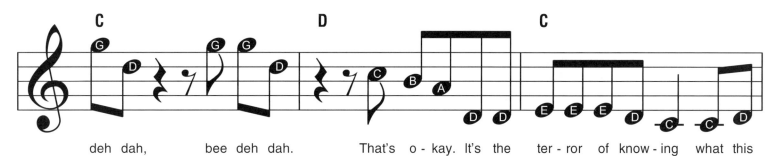

deh dah, bee deh dah. That's o-kay. It's the ter-ror of know-ing what this

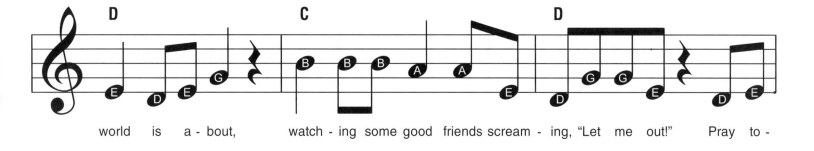

world is a-bout, watch-ing some good friends scream-ing, "Let me out!" Pray to-

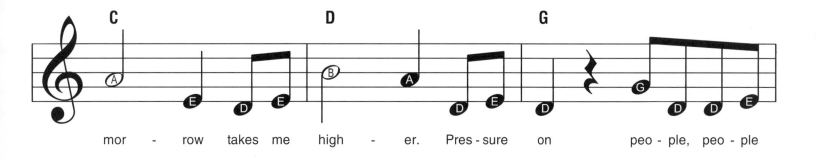

mor-row takes me high-er. Pres-sure on peo-ple, peo-ple

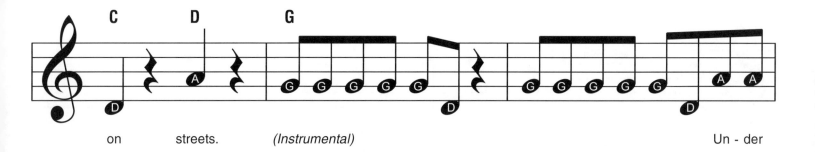

on streets. (Instrumental) Un-der

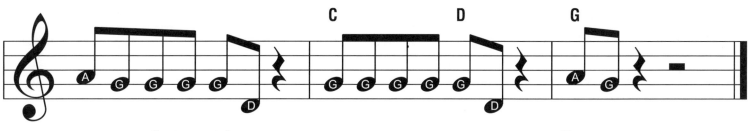

pres-sure. (Instrumental) Pres-sure.

We Are the Champions

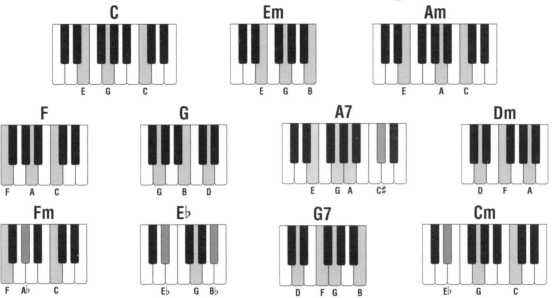

Words and Music by
Freddie Mercury

Moderately slow, in 1

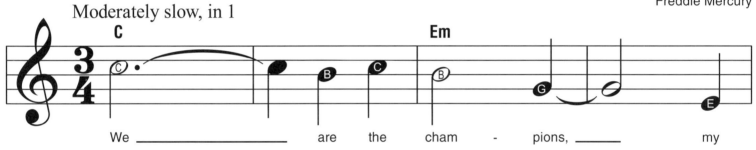

We _____ are the cham - pions, _____ my

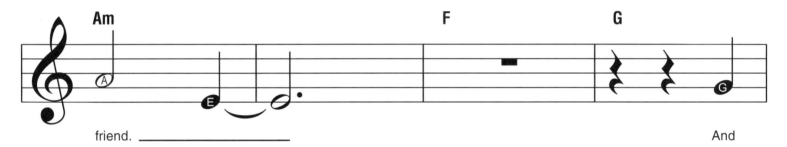

friend. _____ And

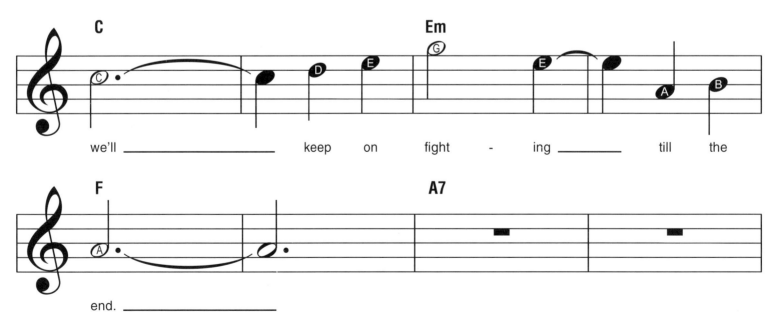

we'll _____ keep on fight - ing _____ till the

end. _____

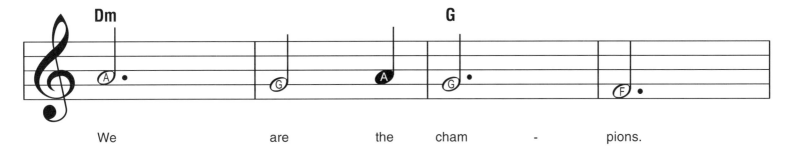

We are the cham - pions.

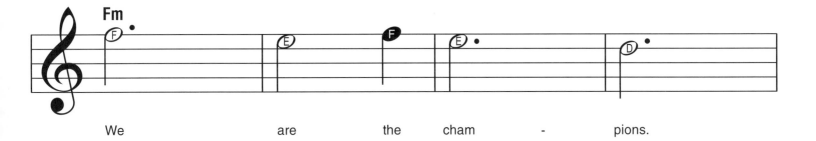

We are the cham - pions.

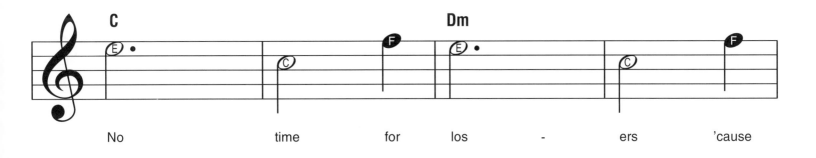

No time for los - ers 'cause

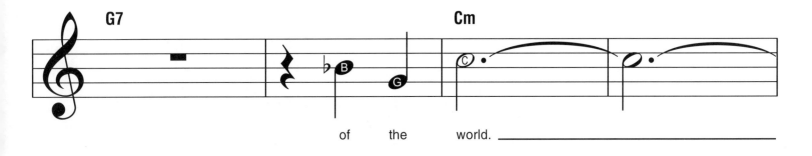

we are the cham - pions

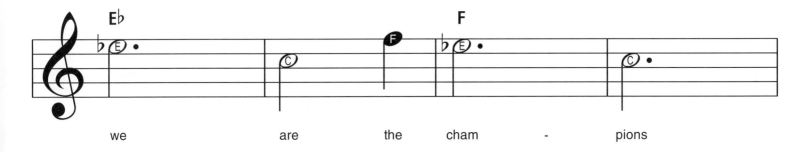

of the world. _____

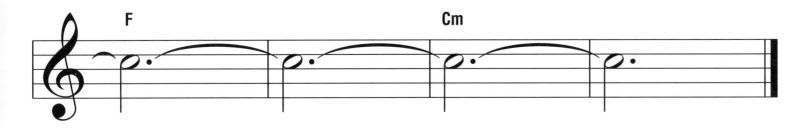

Who Wants to Live Forever

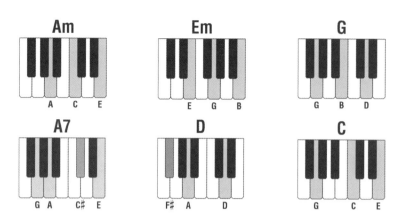

Words and Music by
Brian May

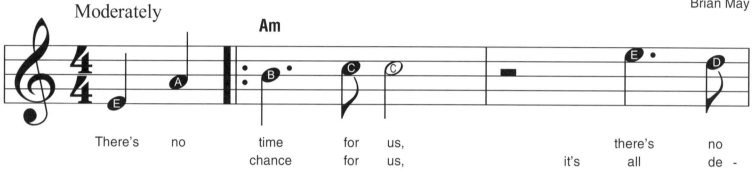

There's   no   time   for   us,   there's   no
chance   for   us,   it's   all   de -

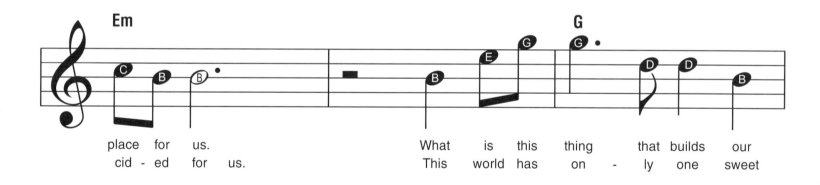

place   for   us.   What   is   this   thing   that   builds   our
cid - ed   for   us.   This   world   has   on - ly   one   sweet

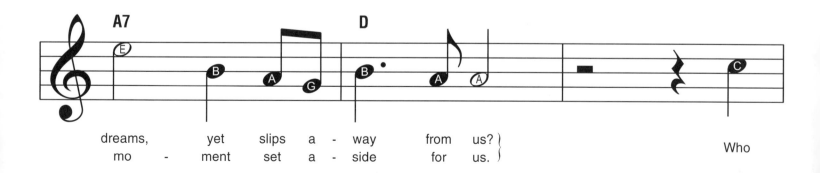

dreams,   yet   slips   a - way   from   us?
mo - ment   set   a - side   for   us.

Who

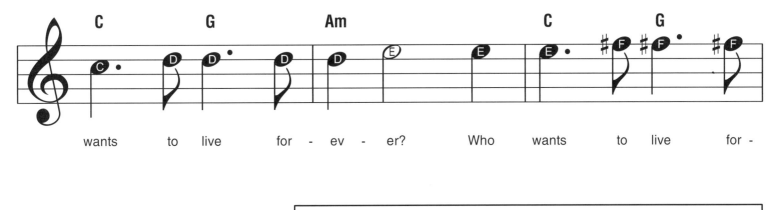

wants   to   live   for - ev - er?   Who   wants   to   live   for -

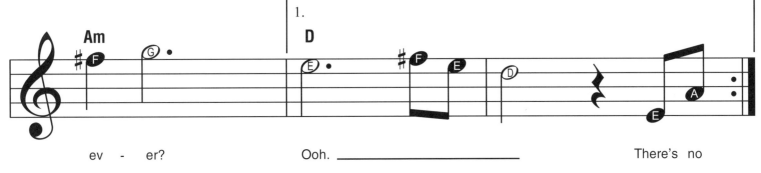

ev - er?   Ooh. _____   There's no

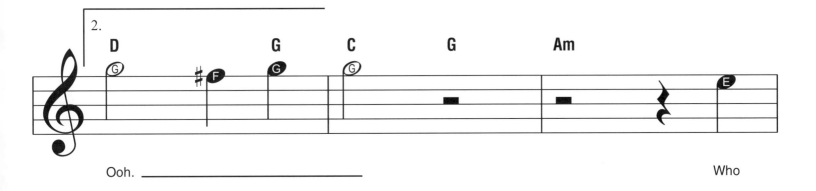

Ooh. _____   Who

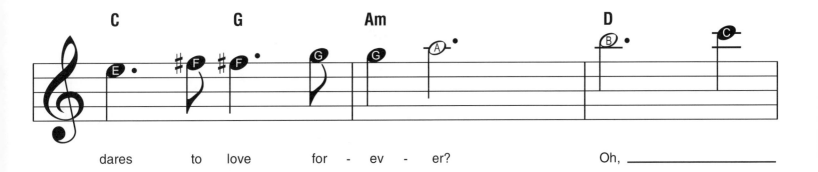

dares   to   love   for - ev - er?   Oh, _____

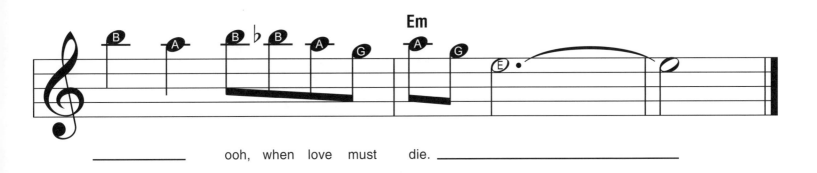

_____ ooh, when love must die. _____

You're My Best Friend

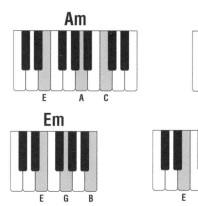
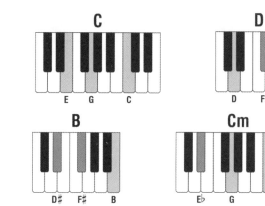
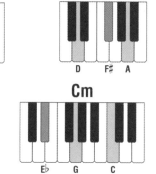

Words and Music by
John Deacon

Moderate Shuffle

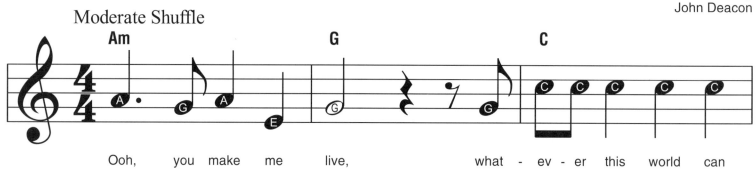

Ooh, you make me live, what-ev-er this world can

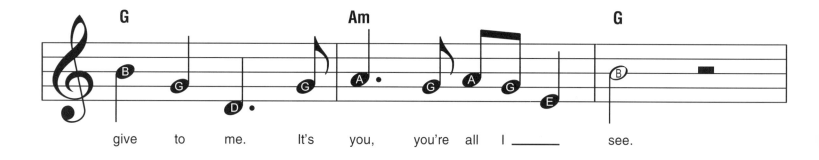

give to me. It's you, you're all I _____ see.

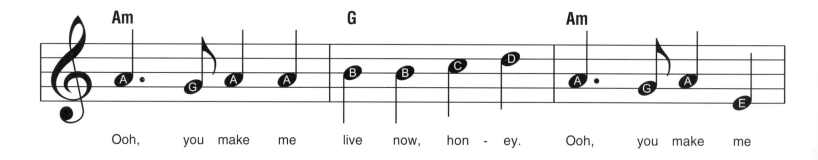

Ooh, you make me live now, hon-ey. Ooh, you make me

live.   Oh, _____ you're the   best   friend   that

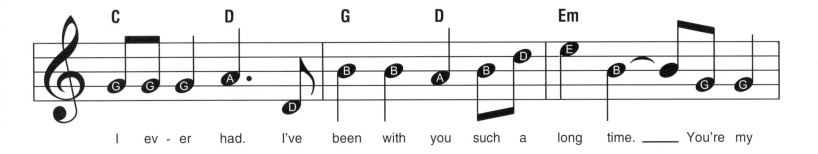

I ev - er had. I've been with you such a long time. _____ You're my

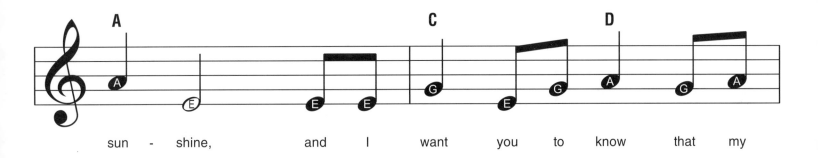

sun - shine,   and   I   want   you   to   know   that   my

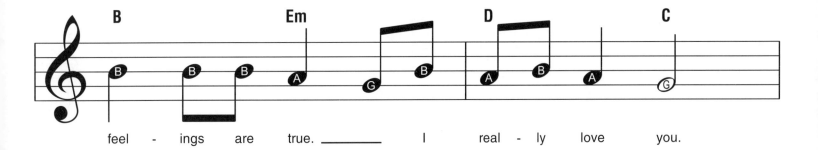

feel - ings are true. _____ I real - ly love you.

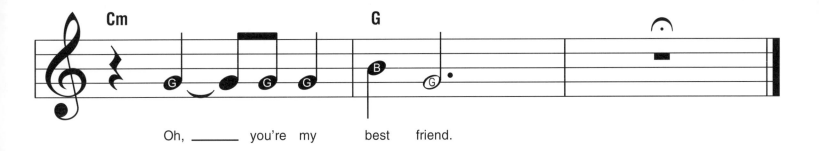

Oh, _____ you're my best friend.

We Will Rock You

Words and Music by
Brian May